MUSEUMS

OF PARIS

MUSEUMS
OF PARIS

AN ILLUSTRATED
GUIDEBOOK TO PARIS MUSEUMS
WITH MAPS, TIME SCHEDULES,
AND RATINGS

Eloise Danto

ELDAN PRESS
Menlo Park, California

LIBRARY OF CONGRESS
CATALOG CARD NO. 87-060214

ISBN - 0 9615128 - 2 - 2

Typography by Laser Express Center, Palo Alto, CA

Cover Design by Michelle Taverniti, San Francisco, CA

Cover Illustrations by Christopher Grubbs, San Francisco, CA

Published by
ELDAN PRESS
1259 El Camino #288
Menlo Park, Ca 94025

TO BRUCE

TABLE OF CONTENTS

INTRODUCTION

It has been said that if all of France's records and archives were destroyed, one could unearth all the information contained therein by visiting the museums of Paris. Paris is felt by many to be the heart of France, and its museums affirm this sentiment. It is more than one of the most exciting cities on earth, more than a center for politics, culture and the arts. Paris is a unique and beautiful city. Its boulevards and avenues are splendidly laid out and the graceful architecture of the past contrasts starkly with the tall and handsome skyscrapers and condominiums of the present. Paris also possesses a distinct artistic charm, a powerful attraction for the discriminating art traveler and museum aficionado. What more could one ask for an incomparable museum setting?

Whereas Florence is affectionately called the Cradle of the Renaissance, Paris is a city of arts and fashion, music, politics and business, romance and intrigue, magic and mystique and, of course, style. The astonishing variety of Parisian museums, from collections of ancient to modern art, science and technology, history, fashion, furnishings, individual artists and the coutless small museums in between, combine to form a tightly knit wealth of unsurpassed art.

To maximize the enjoyment of your museum visits, a few words to the wise are in order regarding transportation. Surface transportation can be considerably trying, so get used to using the Metro. It's the most efficient way to get around. To avoid unnecessary criss-crossing, confine yourself to the museums within one arrondissement (neighborhood) at one time. Also, it is not unusual for some avenues to change names on crossing an intersection, so it's a good idea to focus slightly ahead on your map to avoid overshooting. You should be able to do your own research before setting out on the day's venture, keeping a very clear idea of where you're going and how you plan to get there. Also, get used to carrying your

Plan de Paris par Arrondissement, and Michelin Plan de Paris #10, both available at newsstands and bookstores. To find out when and where special expositions are being held, buy the weekly Pariscope or Officiel des Spectacles, also sold at newsstands. Group shows and current Salons will be listed, as will be limited listings of certain museums.

Generally, opening hours and days remain fairly consistent. However, since it's not unusual for a museum to close suddenly due to a labor problem or malfunction of some sort, it's a good idea to telephone before leaving for your visits. Also, entry prices invariably rise with the passage of time, so make proper allowances.

Remember, 45% of Paris museums are closed on Tuesday, 45% are closed on Monday, just about all are free on Sunday, and those which are not sometimes charge half price. Thus, Sundays are overcrowded not only with international tourists but with French families spending their day enjoying several leisurely museum visits. Once inside the museums you will not find "petite guides" in English, except for the very few popular museums. So be prepared to either use your imagination or do your own translations.

Due to the preponderance of museums and their diversity, I have devised several means of pinpointing and locating them. The first is the Table of Contents, in which they are grouped by arrondissements. The second is the Appendix, in which they are grouped by type. If all else fails, consult the Alphabetical Index, which will surely help to find your museum. Each arrondissement is diagrammed on its own individual page with museums clearly marked and the nearest Metro stations indicated by Ⓜ .

Do not be confused when you see the word "Hotel" written as a listing for a museum. Many 17th century town houses of princes, dukes or duchesses, then know as hotels, were turned into museums, e.g., Carnavalet, Biron, Sevigny and so on. The word "Hotel" simply was never dropped.

My system of star ratings is not based on personal preference but on quality of contents, manner of presentation, lighting, explanations, dating, sense of order, and the degree of professionalism.

As guests of Paris, we should be indebted to that city and to the French government for their reverence of the humanities and the arts, and for their successful restoration endeavors, painstakingly time-consuming and costly processes. We are indeed fortunate to be able to take advantage of this incredible assortment of art from other eras and places.

It is my hope that I have succeeded in bringing to the serious art traveler's attention an awareness of the lesser known and smaller museums of Paris, those containing superb little collections, those in addition to the half-dozen conventionally sought after and heavily trafficked larger ones. Thus, the well-rounded, sophisticated art aficionado is given a rare opportunity for a more sensitive understanding and expansion of his knowledge of other collections and facets of art.

You are now about to embark upon a journey into an incomparable world that many tourists, and even some residents, do not know exists, a voyage of exploration and discovery, your personalized visit to the magnificent museums of Paris.

1st ARRONDISSEMENT

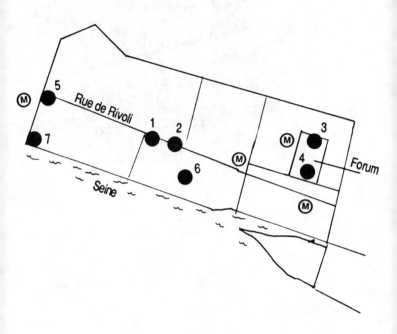

ARTS DECORATIFS

Type:	*Arts*	Open:	*11-5 Daily*
Add:	*107, rue de Rivoli*	Closed:	*Monday & Tuesday*
Tel:	*42.60.32.14*	Entry:	*20 Fr.*
Metro:	*Louvre*	Rating:	*****

No doubt about it, this is the creme de la creme of incredible richness and grandeur, the decorative and ornamental arts, comprising furniture and furnishings of upper-class French life from the Napoleonic First and Second empires through all the Louis's and up to 20th century contemporary. You must appreciate the splendor of each salon, striking and elaborate in its uniqueness. Recent restoration of this five story portion of the Louvre has resulted in a beautifully planned museum of infinitely good taste. Almost the entire collection is permanent. The visitor is never overwhelmed because each of the more than 100 rooms is so self-contained that at no time does one theme spill over to the next. Even the temporary exhibitions are excellent. The museum store on the ground floor offers a better than average collection of postal cards, books and gift items. Arts Decoratifs is outstanding.

ARTS de la MODE

Type:	*Fashion*	Open:	*Wed-Sat- 12:30-6:30*
Add:	*102, rue de Rivoli*		*Sun- 11-5:00*
Tel:	*42.60.32.14*	Metro:	*Palais Royal*
Entry:	*22 Fr.*	Rating:	****

The museum, completed in 1986, is in the outside corner of the Louvre and just next door to the Musee des Arts Decoratifs, entrance on the rue de Rivoli. You must take the elevator up to the fifth floor and from there the expositions are up on the next five levels. Nothing has been spared. This is one of Paris' most well- attended museums, not only by museum goers, but by groups of couturieres from the world over. The treatment of mannequins is unusually done. They are created of fine wood or porcelain, exquisitely painted, then juxtaposed in a most intriguing manner of distinct colorations with dramatically coordinated lighting. Temporary expositions only, recalling the evolution of principally feminine fashion from the 18th century to the present, are shown in supreme extravagance. If fashion is one of your interests this museum must not be missed. It's absolutely visual.

GREVIN

Type: *General*	Entry:	*32 Fr.*
Add: *Forum des Halles*	Metro:	*Chatelet*
Level I #55	Rating:	*
Tel: *42.61.28.50s*		

By now you know this is a wax museum; the entire show represents Paris during its Belle Epoch depicted by twenty lifelike scenes portraying the glittering heros and heroines of that turn of the century era. Models speak, eyes move, clocks tick, dogs bark, music plays and the lights raise and lower, signalling the visitor on to the next scene. The narrative is simple and entertaining. In the Gustave Eiffel scenario, he makes reference to his contribution to the construction of the Statue of Liberty. Farther on, Toulouse Lautrec is sketching, Sarah Bernhardt is dramatizing Cleopatra, and so on. Done in full dramatic bravissimo, the sound effects are charming. The show is slightly corny, but Paris is Paris and wax museums are wax museums. There's another Musee Grevin at 10 Bd. Montmartre where an equally beguiling performance is guaranteed.

MUSEE HOLOGRAPHIE

Type: *Science*
Add: *Forum des Halles*
Level I, # 15-21
Tel: *42.96.96.83*

30-7 *Daily*
1-7 *Sat Sun & Holidays*
Entry: *22 Fr.*
Rating: *

Holographics was invented in the 1940's and is described as a codage of laser lights projected via a system of interferences. Simply put, it is monochromatic light, perfectly regulated in time and space. Different lasers produce different colors. The hologram is the result of two fasciaux from the same source, one direct and the other reflected. This museum exhibits a series of these remarkable three dimensional holographic reflections. As you move across each projected image, that image moves along with you. The sensation of this visual accomplishment is really an exciting mystery. One wonders, does this object that I see really exist? The answer is not at all, it's merely an image. Simple? Although the subject matter is imaginative the museum is unfortunately in shabby condition and poorly maintained.

JEU DE PAUME

Type: *Arts*
Add: *Place de la Concorde*
Tel: *42.60.12.07*
Metro: *Concorde*

Open: *9:45-5:15 Daily*
1:30-5:15 Sat Sun &
Holidays
Entry: *20 Fr.*
Rating: ****

In the late 1870s a small renegade group of painters - Manet, Degas, Sisley, Monet, Pissarro, Renoir, and the American Berthe Morisot - banded together and formed their own movement, called it Impressionism, and revolutionized Western art. Jeu de Paume, the two-storied gallery 500 feet across from the Orangerie, shows the best of these artists and adds to it the Post-Impressionism era of Van Gogh, Cezanne, and others. This is one of the finest collections of its kind, with brilliant pieces coupled with exciting vitality and touching mementos. For a special prize, see the portrait of the rarely painted Emile Zola done by Edouard Manet. In 1986 Jeu de Paume moved all its treasures to the d'Orsay and is scheduled to reopen in 1988 as the Musee d'Art et d'Essai for temporary exhibits.

LOURE

Type: *Arts*	Open: *9:45-5 Daily*
Add: *Palais du Louvre,*	Closed: *Tuesday*
Rue de Rivoli	Entry: *20 Fr.*
Metro: *Louvre*	Rating: ★★★★
Tel: *42.60.39.26*	

The Louvre is unquestionably the finest, most prestigious museum in the world, and retains its undisputed claim as one of Paris' most important public buildings, if not the most popularly attended. It was originally constructed in 1200 as a fortress and was subsequently used as the royal palace. Unfortunately with each successive monarchy the Louvre gradually fell into a shabby state of disrepair until our friend Napoleon, who incidentally was married here, took reconstructive matters into his own hands and commenced bringing the palace up to a new level of grandeur. The Louvre as we know it today was subsequently completed by Baron Haussmann almost seven hundred years after it was begun. The fine arts were placed there by each successive monarchy, thus enriching its fabulous collection over the years. To simplify matters, the Louvre is separated into seven divisions: Greek-Roman, Egyptian, Oriental, Objects of Art, Sculpture, Drawings, and Paintings. Don't expect to view the entire museum in one visit. For that matter, a dozen visits will not complete the entire collection. It might also be a good idea to have your plan of attack well thought out in advance. It is impossible to cite in detail all the works within the Louvre, so for a well rounded outlook you might research the enormous assortment of specialized books. Whereas at one time guided visits were fairly popular, rented cassettes have become more commonplace. At any rate, prepare yourself for a considerable undertaking. There is constant restoration going on somewhere in the Louvre, the most current and sensational being I.M. Pei's gigantic glass pyramid which will be placed over the new entrance directly in the center of the courtyard. This should double the museum's space, and number of the visitors as well. Included in the plans are underground stores, a restaurant, a two level parking lot to accommodate more autos plus dozens of traffic-clogging busses. Allow time for browsing in the museum store which is in itself larger than most museums. It's well laid out and has gift items which range from 25 cent postal cards to $1,500 for copies of works of art within the museum. There's something for everyone here.

L'ORANGERIE

Type: *Arts*
Add: *Place de la Concorde*
Tel: *42.97.48.16*
Metro: *Concorde*

Open: *9:45-5:15 Daily*
Closed: *Tuesday*
Entry: *10 Fr.*
Rating: ******

Since L'Orangerie is adjacent to Jeu de Paume they're considered as sister museums, two stately sentinels guarding the western edge of the Tuilleries. L'Orangerie's permanent collection covers early Impressionism starting with Renoir (some of his most coveted oils are here) through Post Impressionism to Matisse and Picasso, with some excellent Cezannes, Sisleys and others. L'Orangerie, despite the fact that it is one of Paris' smaller museums, is one of the more important ones, particularly since its major refurbishment in 1985. Its salons are large, clean and bright, and displays are considerately placed at eye level. Downstairs, Monet's shimmering Water Lily panels hang in two specially designed oval rooms. If you stand at a distance, these masterpieces are sure to convince you that both the pond and the lillies are moving. This is a must for your itinerary.

2nd ARRONDISSEMENT

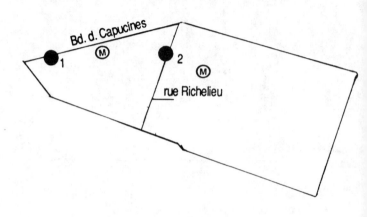

KEY	MUSEUM	PAGE
1.	Cognac Jay	11
2.	Biblioteque National	12

COGNAC JAY

Type:	*Arts*	Open:	*10-5:40 Daily*
Add:	*25, bd. des Capucines*	Closed:	*Monday*
Tel:	*42.61.94.54*	Entry:	*9 Fr.*
Metro:	*Opera*	Rating:	***

At the turn of the 20th century, Ernest Cognac and his wife, Louise Jay, co-founders of the Samaritaine stores in Paris, donated this museum to the city of Paris. Their 18th century mansion which had served as a boutique in the chain held a collection of 17th and 18th century paintings of the highest order (the much admired Lawrence painting, The Calmady Sisters, is here) including Boucher, Tieppolo, Geuze, Chardin and Reynolds. Start at the top floor and work your way down. The furnishings are elegant, and the rich porcelains and miniature boxes of enameled gold and silver are sumptuous. Perhaps due to the small size of its rooms, there are neither large pieces nor large paintings displayed. Even the luxurious tapestries are small. This might explain why almost all the paintings are portraits. The museum is not popular and is infrequently visited.

BIBLIOTEQUE NATIONAL

Type:	*History*	Open:	*1-5 Daily*
Add:	*58, rue Richelieu*	Entry:	*10 Fr.*
Tel:	*42.61.52.83*	Rating:	*
Metro:	*Bourse*		

The National Library is housed in an immense mansion and is said to contain five million books, one hundred thousand manuscripts, two million engravings, a half million maps, and a half million medallions. The library is reputed to be the world's largest and I have no doubt it is. At any given time you will encounter a few hundred students studying there. Two galleries show temporary exhibitions. You will have to look for the museum which is called Musee de Medailles et Antiques, up the broad staircase, through huge doors and on into the large room. Showcases display monies and medals from very early civilizations, jewels, some pottery and antique furnishings. Since most visitors come to use the library, the museum is not well-attended. However, they've done a nice job of identifying their exhibits and there's a new gift shop on the main floor.

3rd ARRONDISSEMENT

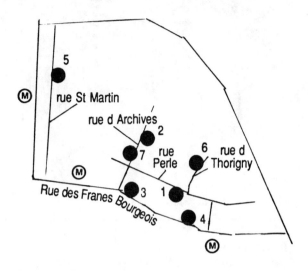

KEY	MUSEUM	PAGE
1.	Bricard de la Serrure	14
2.	Chasse et de la Nature	15
3.	Histoire de France	16
4.	Kwok-On	17
5.	National des Techniques	18
6.	Picasso	19
7.	Musique Mechanique	20

BRICARD de la SERRURE

Type:	*General*	Open:	*10-12/2-5 Daily*
Add:	*1, rue de la Perle*	Closed:	*Sun Mon &*
Tel:	*42.77.79.62*		*Holidays, Month of*
Metro:	*St. Paul*		*August*
Entry:	*10 Fr.*	Rating:	***

In 1872 Eugene Bricard and his sons, who were key manufacturers in Paris, bought this hotel, thereby founding the privileged decorative key business. Pass through the cobblestone courtyard to enter the museum, and up the stairs. All five salons which make up the museum are contained on one floor in this beautifully restored and meticulously maintained residence. Every imaginable lock, key, door knock, door knob and handle, mostly ornamental, are displayed in well marked glass cases; also, bronze and iron locks and keys from Roman, Gothic and Renaissance eras continuing right on up through the 20th century. La Maison Bricard maintains and enjoys its reputation as the most prestigious key maker in the world. The museum is complete with a small garden out back and is just a stone's throw from Picasso and Victor Hugo.

CHASSE et de la NATURE

Type: *General*   Open: *10-5:30 Daily*
Add: *60, rue des Archives*   Closed: *Tues & Holidays*
Tel: *42.72.86.43*   Entry: *10 Fr.*
Metro: *Rambuteau*   Rating: *

There are four floors to this superb mid 1660's hotel (notice
the original staircase as you climb up), and it is beautifully
restored. Located on one of the narrowest streets of the densely
populated Marais it is difficult to spot. Inside are objects and
creatures related uniquely to the hunt - wild animals of all sizes
stuffed and mounted, the larger ones standing about on the
floors, some bronzed, some carved of fine woods, and a
number of skillfully painted life-like decoys. The walls are
filled with drawings and paintings of hounds, hunters, and the
hunted. Tapestries, trophies, guns and weapons adorn the
remaining spaces. Jean-Baptiste Oudry, the most outstanding
painter of nature and animals, is shown and of course the
voluptuous Diana, Goddess of the Hunt, puts in an appearance.
The museum is also a center for an exclusive French hunting
club.

HISTOIRE de FRANCE

Type: *History*
Add: *60, rue des
    Francs-Bourgeois*
Tel: *42.77.11.30*
Metro: *Rambuteau*

Open: *2-5 Daily*
Closed: *Tues & Holidays*
Entry: *4 Fr.*
Rating: ****

The immense riches of the National Archives, formerly the Hotel Soubise, consist of authentic documents, from Charlemagne's college diploma to Napoleon's will and Marie Antoinette's last written letter. Exhibits cover the history of France from the Middle Ages to World War II, her tumultuous struggles, social reforms, political protestations, the Revolution, France's capture of North Africa in the mid 1880's, a miniature stone model of the Bastille, remarkably the only one I've seen in Paris, an exhibit of proposed underwater exploration, circa 1715, and drawings of a submarine, 1689! By the way, there really was a Princess of Soubise. She lived here in this splendid 18th century mansion. The bed she slept in, although a little shabby, is still properly made.

KWOK-ON

Type: *Oriental*
Add: *41, rue des Francs-Bourgeois*
Tel: *42.72.99.42*
Metro: *St. Paul*

Open: *12-6 Daily*
Closed: *Sat & Sun*
Entry: *10 Fr.*
Rating: ***

Critically speaking this is not really a museum. It's a limited exhibition in a pretty barren setting of the private collection of Mr. Kwok-On, whomever he may be, who held a fascination for ritualistic masks, and there are hundreds displayed here. All are of Chinese origin from the 11th, 12th, and 13th centuries, ranging from masks of exorcism used to chase devils and other harmful influences to elaborate masks for propitiation of gods and favorable influences. There are no simple masks. Each one is complex and exotically hand crafted from feathers to woods to porcelains. The showcases are against the walls, well lit but explanations are brief or sketchy and the museum is somewhat shabby. If you're an Oriental mask enthusiast you'll love Kwok-On, for that's all there is.

NATIONAL des TECHNIQUES

Type: *Science*
Add: *270, rue St. Martin*
Tel: *42.71.24.14*
Metro: *Arts et Metiers*

Open: *1-5 Daily*
      10-5 Sunday
Closed: *Monday*
Entry: *10 Fr.*
Rating: ********

This is one of the most amazing museums in Paris and surely one of the largest, sizewise and otherwise. It appears that part of the building was a 14th century priory and cathedral, a remarkable setting for a science museum containing invented and perfected science and technology from a 5th century wheel to a steam auto (1770), steamboats, a helicopter (1905), trains and locomotives, the first French airplane (1906), the theory of windmill power and an incredible assortment of machines, some working and all explained in intricate detail. And three more floors of mind boggling intricacies: glass making, sound systems, electronic measuring devices, and on and on. The horlogerie (clock) collection is one of the most celebrated in the world. The intelligence contained here is limitless. If you are an admirer of theory and technology prepare to spend a long, exhausting and rewarding day.

PICASSO

Type:	*Artist*	Open:	*10-5:15 Daily*
Add:	*5, rue de Thorigny*		*10-10 Wed*
Tel:	*42.71.25.21*	Closed:	*Tuesday*
Metro:	*St. Paul*	Entry:	*20 Fr.*
		Rating:	****

Several years of negotiation and extensive restoration have proven to be more than worthwhile. The elegantly restored 17th century Hotel Sale opened in 1985 to rave notices, and it's easy to see why. No doubt about it, Picasso, who died in 1973, revolutionized 20th century art. Wasn't it Pablo who said, "Give me a museum and I will fill it". Who can describe such power and from wherein comes this depth? This is an important museum that is as close to perfection as one can get. Covering all phases of his career, salon after salon, floor after floor, there are almost 3,000 of his gem-like works that personify the talent of this genius with incredible intensity. Those canvasses by Matisse and Degas are from Picasso's private collection. Be sure to visit the sculpture garden in the inner courtyard for some dazzling pieces that literally transcend all time and language. The Hotel Sale is an absolute must on your museum itinerary.

MUSIQUE MECHANIQUE

Type: *Music*
Add: *Impasse Berthaud*
Tel: *42.71.99.54*
Metro: *Rambuteau*

Open: *2-7 Sat Sun & Holidays*
Entry: *10 Fr.*
Rating: ***

Mechanical music enjoyed brief popularity from the early
1800's to the early 1900's. The museum is really the
extraordinary collection (and the only one in Paris) of M. et
Mme. Triquet, either one of whom will conduct a personalized
demonstration tour lasting an hour and a half. There are four
small rooms which cover an immense variety of mechanical
pianolas, polyphones, music boxes, musicians and dancers,
mostly made in France, and all in perfect working order. There
are automatic circus pipe organs and accordians. And notice
the irresistable mechanical tree of singing birds. The
phonograph room tells about the birth of recorded sound and
explains of the mathematical principles of piano rolls and
cylinders. There's also a working model of a stereo system,
1890. Bravo for a refreshing visit.

4th ARRONDISSEMENT

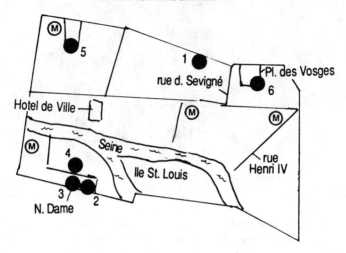

CARNAVALET

Type:	*History*	Open:	*10-5:40 Daily*
Add:	*23, rue de Sevigne*	Closed:	*Monday*
Tel:	*42.72.21.13*	Entry:	*12 Fr.*
Metro:	*St. Paul*	Rating	*

If crowds at the Louvre distress you, visit this hotel in the center of the Marais for some firsthand insights into the life and breadth of Paris during all her periods from the 17th to the 19th centuries visualized through paintings, drawings, letters, etchings and memorabilia. It is actually the Museum of the City of Paris and quite exciting at that. The Louis XVI wing is particularly elegant. Whose attache case lies on the small table in Salle 57? And visit the apartments of the daring and illustrious Mme. Sevigny who achieved a formidable amount of notoriety during her stay here. And glance down into the several lovely courtyards, particularly the one the entry with its curious center sculpture. Carnavalet, with all its vivacity, is in need of restoration.

CATHEDRAL NOTRE DAME

Type:	*History*	Open:	*10-5 Daily*
Add:	*Sq. Notre Dame*	Entry:	*Free*
Tel:	*43.26.07.39*	Rating:	******
Metro:	*Cite*		

Notre Dame Cathedral is one of the most outstanding
examples of 12th century Gothic architecture in Europe. The
Cathedral deteriorated over the centuries and was restored to its
proper majestic status by Napoleon during his reign. This was
actually the site of a temple to Jupiter during the Roman
Empire. Suffice it to say there have been so many volumes
written on Notre Dame that they could fill a hundred libraries.
One must visit it, not only for what it is but for what it
represents. No doubt the reading of Victor Hugo's "The
Hunchback of Notre Dame" will lend sensitive and moving
insight into Paris' history and the role of Notre Dame in that
history. Also, since the Ile de la Cite was of major
geographical importance to the city of Paris, the cathedral quite

naturally played a dominant role in all its political and social affairs, such as invocations, proclamations, and, of course, Napoleon's coronation in 1804. Free guided tours are given daily and, if you feel able, you can ascend the towers where an assortment of friendly gargoyles awaits your arrival at the very top. Vast numbers of tourists are constantly gathered here. No matter, the Cathedral is so enormous that even if it were filled one would not feel crowded. You have not completed your visit to Paris until you have walked through Notre Dame.

CRYPTE NOTRE DAME

Type: *Natural History*   Open: *10-5:30 Daily*
Add: *Parvis de Notre Dame* Entry: *9 Fr.*
Tel: *43.29.83.51*
Metro: *Cite*

Here is bona fide evidence of the Roman Empire civilization which flourished in Paris and remained undiscovered for 15 centuries. The story begins in 300 B.C. when, due to its proximity to the seine, the Ile de la Cite was the primary site of paris' defense forces. The crypte was actually a group of homes, shops and military quarters for the city. apartments and paths beneath are intact, complete with intricate heating systems, pretty sophisticated testimonial for the times. In 1986 while digging for additional parking facilities, further portions of the crypte were unearthed. If you are interested in archaeological ruins, the crypte is worth a visit. Its presentation is extraordinarily well documented and chronological diagrams and explanations are translated into English. Naturally, the awesome cathedral goes along with this visit.

MUSEE NOTRE DAME

Type: *History*
Add: *10, rue du*
    Cloitre Notre Dame
Tel: *43.25.42.92*

Metro: *Cite*
  Open: *2:30-6 Wed Sat Sun*
Entry: *10 Fr.*
Rating: *

Most people are unaware of this museum's existence. It's across the street and along the side of the Cathedral, tucked quietly in between two buildings. The contents within its two rooms contain drawings, paintings, engravings, lithographs and manuscripts, all relating to the creation of Notre Dame and the spectacular events which took place over the centuries since the 11th century when Notre Dame was constructed. You'll see baptisms, marriages, funerals, and Te Diums in glorious pomp and pageantry, along with portraits of past Archbishops and religious leaders, and monies, pottery, and jewelry found in the Crypte beneath the Cathedral. No English brochure is available, so you're in for some difficult translation.

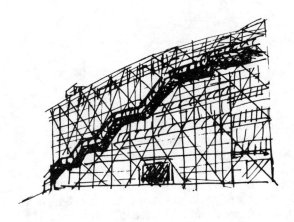

GEORGES POMPIDOU

Type:	*Arts*	Open:	*12-10 Daily*
Add:	*rue Rambuteau*	Closed:	*Tuesday*
Tel:	*47.77.12.33*	Entry:	*20Fr.*
Metro:	*Rambuteau*	Rating:	****

The epitome of revolutionary Avant Garde in visual arts, Beaubourg, as it is affectionately called, opened in the late 1970's to a shocked Paris and still remains one of its most controversial creations and a major attraction of the city. Its gaudy main escalator in brightly colored plastic angles up the five story facade alongside of walking galleries and giant colored tubes used for containing water and heat, a telephone system, plumbing and ventilation. The founder, former President Georges Pompidou, envisioned not only a museum to contain conventional paintings and sculptures, but a complete cultural center. And that's what Beaubourg is. The Museum of Modern Art on the third and fourth floors is reputedly the largest in the world. There's an enormous, well-equipped public library, a museum of graphics, design and architecture, a branch of the French Film Library which contains its own auditorium, movie theatre and musical laboratory, and a lively and innovative childrens workshop/play center. The Industrial Design Center is in a gallery on the second floor and exhibits something unusual, an ideally planned environmental community. Temporary exhibitions are on the fifth floor. Maestro Pierre Boulez also conducts guest concert appearances in one of the theatres. You will find one of the best and largest museum shops in Paris on the ground floor. If all this culture exhausts you, escalate on up to the crowded fifth floor restaurant for a refreshing snack and a panoramic view of Paris. Beaubourg, in the beloved Les Halles section of Paris, with its transparent walls and miles of multi-colored stairwells, is without doubt an influential forerunner of the changing face of Paris. Witness the architecture of its immediate neighborhood.

VICTOR HUGO

Type:	*Individual*	Open:	*10-5:40 Daily*
Add:	*6, Place des Vosges*	Closed:	*Monday*
Tel:	*42.72.16.65*	Entry:	*15 Fr.*
Metro:	*Chemin Vert*	Rating:	***

Thanks to the Friends of Victor Hugo here's a beautifully
restored hotel. And what a treat to visit the rich, elegant
living quarters where the Hugos lived. Hugo was a man of
formidable wealth and the museum's contents have been
gathered from several of his homes. He was politically active
and a member of Parliament, during which time he wrote
several papers on human rights. He also possessed a biting,
witty sense of humor seen in his caricatures. He prolifically
painted in water color and masterfully designed pieces of
complex woodworked furnishings. How he loved interior
designing! Dozens of family portraits adorn the walls along
with drawings and photos done by Mrs. Hugo, apparently an
accomplished artist also. Can you find Mr. Hugo in the group
drawing of "guests" in the Pantheon? Second row, third from
left. There's an awesome sense of silence in this dynamic
museum. Do visit it.

5th ARRONDISSEMENT

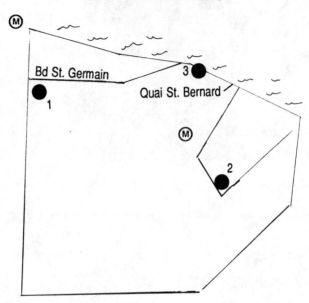

KEY	MUSEUM	PAGE

CLUNY

Type:	*History*	Open:	*9:45-12:30/2-5 Daily*
Add:	*6, Place Paul-Painleve*	Closed:	*Tuesday*
Tel:	*43.25.62.00*	Entry:	*16 Fr.*
Metro:	*St. Michel*	Rating:	*****

Cluny, one of the most popular museums in Paris, appears to be another of the rare remaining evidences of a flourishing community of the Roman Empire (see Crypte, Notre Dame). In the 15th century, a private manor was built over the Roman ruins and what you see are the remains of both. This is no doubt the only museum in Paris containing medieval artifacts exclusively. Since you're at the bottom, simply start there, at the thermes (thermal baths). On the main floor there are hundreds of miniature ivories and wooden figures and alabaster friezes on the walls. Upstairs are religious carvings, paintings, stained glass windows, an incredibly large assortment of tapestries and, of course, in a special salon the celebrated six Woman and Licorne tapestries, artist(s) unknown. Cluny draws large crowds, probably because it's also a spiritual museum.

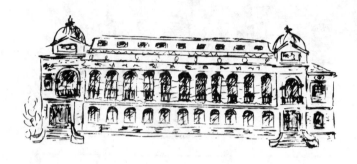

HISTOIRE NATURELLE

Type:	*Natural History*	Open:	*1:30-5 Daily*
Add:	*57, rue Cuvier*	Closed:	*Tues & Holidays*
Tel:	*43.31.89.59*	Entry:	*16 Fr. - Gardens Free*
Metro:	*Jussieu*	Rating:	**

The museum is composed of six huge buildings along one side
of the gardens: zoology, biology, anatomy, minerology, and
so on. At the head of the broad central path is an enormous
building for expositions pertaining to the natural sciences.
The gardens were originally planted early in the 17th century
for the cultivation of medicinal herbs and later landscaped into
wide avenues geometrically laid out with hundreds of flower
beds, plants and trees, surely as aesthetic as the famous gardens
of Luxembourg. And a splendid zoo, too. The museum, its
gardens and zoo have become a national institution for most
Parisian families, a means of spending the entire day here, then
back to the chaos of the city. That huge acacia tree you see in
the center path really is 350 years old.

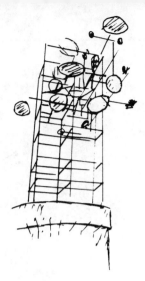

SCULPTURE PLEIN AIR

Type: *Arts*   Open: *Year Round*
Add: *Quai St. Bernard*   Entry: *Free*
Metro: *Jussieu*   Rating: ****

You needn't concern yourself about the opening or closing
hours, or days for that matter. This is called a public art
museum and it's open day and night year round. Why, it's
even lit up at night. There are a dozen or so outdoor
sculptures in bronze, iron, granite and marble interspersed
throughout this three-acre park which sits on the west bank of
the Seine. The city of Paris has thoughtfully provided plenty
of sitting space for this new and innovative concept, also
known as Architectural Art. From this vantage point, you'll
see to your left the 13th to 17th century landscape of Ile de la
Cite and Ile St. Louis, then to your right in startling contrast
are the skyscrapers of modern downtown Paris This is a clean,
classy, and well maintained museum and it's all free.

6th ARRONDISSEMENT

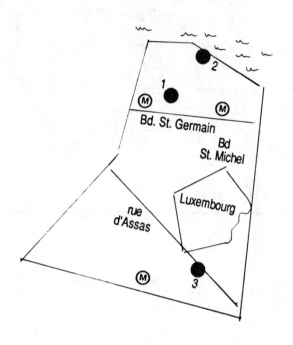

EUGENE DELACROIX

Type: *Artist*
Add: *6, Place Furstenburg*
Tel: *43.54.04.87*
Metro: *St. Germain-des-Pres*

Open: *9:45-5 Daily*
Closed: *Tues & Holidays*
Entry: *12 Fr.*
Rating: *******

This lovely pink stucco three-story museum is tucked into an intimate square behind the chaotic Boulevard St. Germain. It's the apartment and atelier where Delacroix lived, worked, and died and is filled with his exciting drawings, oils, water colors and pastels, all clearly identified. Take the small door out where a sign reads, "atelier" to get to his studio, where he particularly enjoyed painting scenes from literature and the Bible. Did you notice his paint boxes set into specially built tables and his personal belongings in the glass cases? It is easy to see why Delacroix was and still is one of the world's favorite romantic painters. How fortunate we are to be able to enjoy not only one of Paris' best small museums, but, for a final touch, there's another private park and garden out back.

MONNAIE

Type:	*General*	Open:	*11-5 Daily*
Add:	*11, Quai Conti*	Metro:	*Odeon*
Tel:	*43.29.12.48*	Closed:	*Sun & Holidays*
Entry:	*10 Fr.*	Rating:	***

The hotel, placed directly on and overlooking the Seine has
Louis XVI's gorgeous flamboyance. Unfortunately, only a
small portion of the splended mansion is maintained for use as
a museum; the remainder houses government offices. The
contents are uniquely hand crafted commemorative coins and
medals, medallions and honorary decorations fabricated in
honor of prominent French figures of arts and letters, historic
occasions, or important social events from the 17th century to
the present. Rare samples of French currency from antiquity
to current times are also shown. However, poor interior
lighting leaves something to be desired and not all displays are
clearly marked. Duplicates of medals are available for
purchase. Just follow the signs, "l'atelier", the workshop.
Although some fine temporary exhibitions are held the
museum is not a popular attraction.

ZADKINE

Type:	*Artist*	Open:	*12-3 Daily*
Add:	*100 bis, rue d'Assas*	Closed:	*Monday*
Tel:	*43.26.91.90*	Entry:	*15 Fr.*
Metro:	*Vavin*	Rating:	***

You're going to have to search for this one. The entrance is in an alley squeezed between two buildings. Ossip Zadkine, a 20th century Russian sculptor, worked not with the conventional chisel as other sculptors, but with saw and hammer, creating baroque-like figures, somewhat like decorative cubism and yet sensuously curvacious. There must be hundreds of sculptures crowded into the museum's four small rooms. Some of his works faintly resemble Leger, some the lyricism of Modigliani. Nestled amongst this jumbled mass of figures and heads are photos of the artist and his family. The small garden out front, referred to as the Sculpture Forest, is abundantly overflowing with figures. Zadkine is virtually unknown in the English speaking world and deserves to be better appreciated. This is certainly an unusual, delightful museum visit.

7th ARRONDISSEMENT

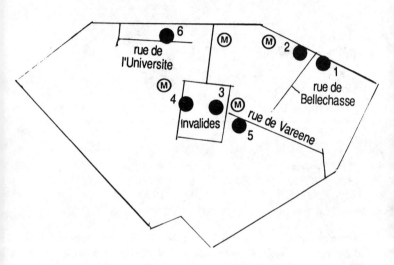

D'ORSAY

Type: *Arts*
Add: *15, rue de Bellechasse*
Tel: *45.44.41.85*
Metro: *Solferino*

Open: *10-5:30 Daily*
Closed: *Tues & Holidays*
Entry: *20 Fr.*
Rating: ******

This was the elegant Belle Epoque railway station, the Gare d'Orsay, built for the 1900 Paris World's Fair. The handsome station actually ceased operating as a rail center in early 1973 and how fortunate for us it escaped demolition. Its original arched ceiling made of thousands of pieces of glass remain. Its massive interior, said to be larger than the Cathedral of Notre Dame, was redesigned by Mme. G. Aulenti, an Italian architect who also renovated the Pompidou. The museum opened late in 1986 and is sensational, the contents gathered from Impressionist collections in Paris from Jeu de Paume, The Palais de Tokyo, the Louvre, and the Musee Arts Decoratifs. From the Carpeaux sculpture gallery in the center, complimented by sculptures by Rodin, Daumier, Degas and

Bourdelle, to the paintings galleries with their broad surrounding balconies, and Art Nouveau salons in between, it's a rare privelege to be treated to the likes of a museum such as this with its luscious paintings, sculpture, architecture, furniture, photography and design. No doubt d'Orsay's incredible size and space contribute to this luxurious feeling. The extraordinary collection here constitutes works of art from the second half of the 19th century, oddly enough, from 1848 to 1914, a fairly brief lapse of time. Several salons are devoted to the display of stained glass and pottery, architecture and furniture, and look for the Paris planning projects by Baron Haussmann, the controversial architect who changed the face of this city. There's a theatre which holds concerts, a section devoted to the opera, another for the decorative arts, and a photography display. For a great bird's eye landscape, the cafe upstairs offers an exceptional view of Paris looking east. D'Orsay must be regarded as one of the most outstanding art experiences in Paris.

LEGION d'HONNEUR

Type:	*Military*	Open:	*2-5 Daily*
Add:	*2, rue de Bellechasse*	Closed:	*Monday*
Tel:	*45.55.95.16*	Entry:	*6 Fr.*
Metro:	*Solferino*	Rating:	***

On entering this small museum a brief film is shown on France's military history and the contents of the galleries within. The medal of The Legion of Honor was created by Napoleon in the early 1800's simply because he insisted on properly honoring his country's heroes. You'll see paintings, etchings and drawings of ceremonies bestowing honors upon exceptional French military leaders and outstanding foreign heroes with the Grand Ordre de la Chevalerie. There are even a few decorated heroines! Plenty of military attire and costumes, ribbons, medals and decorations. All displays are well done. The museum also holds temporary exhibitions of excellent quality, not necessarily of a military nature. Remember the subject matter is limited.

MUSEE de l'ARMEE

Type: *Military*   Open: *10-5 Daily*
Add: *Hotel des Invalides* Closed: *Tuesdays & Holidays*
Tel: *45.55.92.30*   Entry: *16 Fr.*
Metro: *Latour-Maubourg*

Enter through an enormous cobblestoned courtyard where, throughout France's history, all major military events took place, and still do. The museum contains precisely what its name implies: three floors of three wings of Les Invalides filled with historical data of military memorabilia. Aside from centuries of local wars, France has suffered through two World Wars and the museum gives superb coverage of all, complete with inspiring photographs, drawings, flags, medals, costumes, weaponry and armor. Recognition is given to all countries that helped France through all her wars. The Grand Emperor rests in a splendid tomb under the dome surrounded by grandiose chapels and other great war heroes. The museum is remarkably well attended: national pride predominates the atmosphere. Yes, that is La Marseilleaise being piped in and visitors are quick to respond, humming for honor and country.

ORDRE de la LIBERATION

Type:	*Military*	Open:	*2-5 Daily*
Add:	*Hotel des Invalides*	Closed:	*Sunday*
Tel:	*47.05.04.10*	Entry:	*11 Fr.*
Metro:	*Latour-Maubourg*	Rating:	**

This is a small gallery located in the eastern wing of Invalides, enter from the outside. Dedicated to the Resistance movement, the Free French Forces and all who participated in the subsequent liberation of France during World War II, the museum is hardly visited, even by the French population. It seems that very few people know of its existence. The majority of small rooms hold showcases with letters of commendation, proclamations, ordinances, photos, personal memoirs, letters and drawings. The Salle d'Honneur pays tribute to Charles de Gaulle. On the upper floor is a sad memorial in frightening testimony to France's 250 thousand Jews deported to concentration camps never to return. Drawings of survivors in tender poignancy act as reminder to an incredibly terrible time in history. France does not refer to the Holocaust per se, it is spoken of as the Deportation.

MUSEE RODIN

Type:	*Artist*	Open:	*10-5*
Add:	*77, rue de Varenne*	Closed:	*Tuesday*
Tel:	*47.05.01.34*	Entry:	*15 Fr.*
Metro:	*Varenne*	Rating:	****

Prepare yourself for a sublime experience. There are more
Rodin pieces under one roof (and outside) than anywhere else
in the world. His sculpture somehow leaves one quite at a
loss for words. I will therefore let the museum speak for itself
and the visitor can ponder over how any one person could
possibly have accomplished all this. Room after room holds
superb bronze and marble heads, figures and portions of
figures. Rodin apparently was a man of formidable size, per
the portraits by Andre Sinet and Avrigdor, both on the first
floor. The hotel itself is maintained in the same state it was
when Rodin lived here until his death in 1916, with its high
Corinthian columns ascending from richly paneled floors to
elaborately decorated ceilings and stately marble fireplaces
placed along the walls. There are twenty rooms in this

mansion, all filled with Rodin through each of his periods:
marbles, woods, bronzes, ceramics, and of course his drawings.
Oddly enough, the Hotel Biron has enjoyed the presence of a
number of prominent temporary residents. Jean Cocteau,
Henri Matisse, and Isadora Duncan all lived here briefly. A
stroll through the sculpture gardens is an absolute must.
Broad paths and plenty of benches are offered with the dome of
Les Invalides looming overhead just next door. There's a
snack bar off to one side. That's a good idea, since it's no easy
task to tear oneself away from this setting. The small
museum store should be visited for photos, posters, books and
cards that are not to be found anywhere else. These must be
carried back home. Your trip to the museums of Paris is not
complete without stopping here.

SEITA

Type:	*Social*	Open:	*11-6*
Add:	*12, rue Surcouf*	Closed:	*Sun & Holidays*
Tel:	*45.55.91.50*	Entry:	*Free*
Metro:	*Invalides*	Rating:	****

According to SEITA, the official tobacco organization of France, tobacco originated in the US and was brought back to Europe by Columbus. This small museum exhibits the resulting multi-varied products: pipes from all cultures, tobacco holders, chewing tobacco, snuff and its proper use, cigars, smoking apparel, smoking chairs and furnishings, and, of course, the ultimate cigarette. There's some anti-smoking literature from the 19th century from members of the French medical profession and anti- smoking groups arguing the health hazards of smoking, but by this time, alas, smoking had become a glamorous and major part of our social system. A tiny two-seat theatre regularly shows short films on the accepted seductivity of smoking. Another section of the SEITA Museum devotes itself to temporary exhibits of contemporary artists.

8th ARRONDISSEMENT

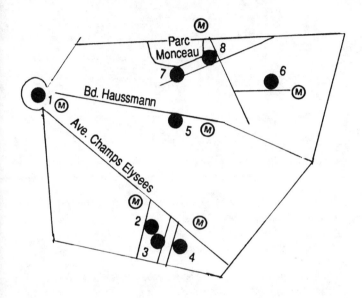

KEY	MUSEUM	PAGE

ARC DE TRIOMPHE

Type:	*History*	Open:	*10-6 Daily*
Add:	*Place Chas. de Gaulle*	Closed:	*Tues & Holidays*
Tel:	*43.80.31.31*	Entry:	*10 Fr.*
Metro:	*Chas. de Gaulle-Etoile*	Rating:	**

To get to the museum take the elevator (when it works) or, if you're feeling particularly energetic, climb the stairs. There's a large room at the middle level which is the museum - it's really a display of pictures and drawings pertaining to the design and building of the Arc, and the spectacles and events that have taken place under it since 1810. In a small room a film is shown which portrays the Arc as an imposing symbol of France, her heroes and her honor. Appropriately, the Arc is the center from which twelve of Paris' main streets radiate. Thus, the Arc de Triomphe has become, in a sense, the heart of Paris. Visiting heads of state pass here; the Tomb of the Unknown Soldier is at its base. Some great moments of French history are recorded at the Arc. For example, in 1885 Victor Hugo was given a memorable funeral attended by two million people. Why was he later removed and placed within the Pantheon?

DECOUVERT

Type:	*Science*	Open:	*10-6 Daily*
Add:	*Ave. Franklin*	Closed:	*Monday*
	Roosevelt	Entry:	*11 Fr.*
	(Grand Palais)	Rating:	****
Tel:	*43.59.16.65*		
Metro:	*Franklin Roosevelt*		

It is impossible to describe all the contents of this museum's sixty salons. It's the most complete collection of cultural scientific information and study anywhere and is presented to the visitor in participatory experiments. What fun with tricks-of-the-eye tests, a paradise of discoveries and creative, mind-boggling adventures. There are daily demonstrations, films and lectures. Some of the subjects explored are telecommunications, medical discoveries and health care, astrology, anthropology, environment, zoology, mineralogy, space travel, maritime exploration, political views, atomic principles, nuclear information, mathematics, theoretical abstractions, cosmic odyssys, a chemical laboratory and on and on. Stop at the fabulous museum store on your way out. A large portion of Decouvert is planned for transference to La Villette in 1988. Definitely exciting!

GRAND PALAIS

Type: *General*   Open: *10-8 Daily*
 Add: *Ave. du General*   Closed: *Tuesday*
     Eisenhower   Entry: *20 Fr.*
 Tel: *42.56.09.24*   Rating: ******
Metro: *Champs Elysees-Clemenceau*

The Grand Palais was designed for the 1900 Paris World's Fair
in an architectural design similar to the Petit Palais across the
street. Both are intimate, elaborate and splendid. At the
present time Grand Palais is primarily open to expositions
which generally stay for between one to three months. Any
exposition held at Grand Palais is meticulously planned and
guaranteed to be a smash hit. Its huge salons accommodate
oversized paintings and visitors are able to sit on comfortable
benches plentifully placed throughout. Large sums of money
are expended for these superb shows, thus drawing wide appeal,
so be prepared for crowds. The west wing contains a
planetarium (extra admission) and the exciting Decouvert (extra
admission). If, during your stay in Paris, Grand Palais is
holding an exposition, it is imperative that you visit it.

PETIT PALAIS

Type: *General*
Add: *Ave. Winston Churchill*
Tel: *42.65.12.73*
Metro: *Champs Elysees-
Clemenceau*

Open: *10-5:40 Daily*
Closed: Monday
Entry: *15 Fr.*
Rating: ****

The glamorous Petit Palais, along with its sister The Grand
Palais, was constructed for the 1900 World's Fair and has since
become known as Paris' Museum of Fine Arts (Beaux Arts).
It is of splendid architecture and its salons and galleries are
truly palatial. The permanent collection is rich and varied with
an assortment of paintings, furnishings, an incredible
Carpeaux sculpture gallery not to be missed, a tapestry gallery,
and a large collection of paintings of the Masters. Each epoch
of art is given its own salon and all are placed neatly in order.
All works are allowed maximum space giving an uncrowded,
luxurious feeling and what better way to properly appreciate all
this fabulous art? Exhibitions are constantly held and there's
plenty of bench space amongst the fountains and flower beds
in the inner courtyard.

JAQUEMART ANDRE

Type:	*General*	Open:	*1:30-5:30 Daily*
Add:	*158 Bd. Haussmann*	Closed:	*Sun Mon & Holidays*
Tel:	*45.51.82.42*	Entry:	*12 Fr.*
Metro:	*Miromesnil*	Rating:	***

In 1870 Edouard Andre, a banker, married Nelie Jaquemart, a painter and fellow patron of the arts. They built this Louis XVI hotel and filled it with the fabulous art treasures found here. The hotel, intact with its original gilt walls paneled with tapestries, gorgeous ceilings and Louis XVI furnishings, serves as an aesthetic background for an extraordinary collection of portraits on the main floor. Upstairs the Andre's 15th and 16th century Italian Renaissance paintings and furnishings plus luscious French art treasures of the Masters absolutely radiate. There are three additional points of particular interest here. First, the Grand Staircase which overlooks the entry foyer; second, the inner doorway entrances, no two of which are alike; and third, those heavenly Tieppolo ceilings. Despite the rich and voluptuous sensation throughout, this museum is sadly in need of restoration.

MUSIQUE CONSERVATOIRE

Type:	*Music*	Open:	*2-5: 30 W-T-F- S*
Add:	*14, rue de Madrid*	Closed:	*S-M-T & Holidays*
Tel:	*42.93.15.20*	Entry:	*7 Fr.*
Metro:	*Europe*	Rating:	****

The Conservatory of Music is just one-half block down from the Metro. Once inside, signs will point you to Le Musee, a small one-room charmer which is certain to arouse your classical sensivities. Great effort must be exerted to not reach out to touch these delicate hand painted harpsichords, clavichords, lutes, 17th century guitars, mandolins, lyres, violins, and double keyboard pianos. Is it possible the giant octobass at the entry is still playable? We are so fortunate in being given an opportunity to glimpse into the private world of so few gifted and dedicated musicians. It's no small wonder about the immense popularity that this tiny museum attracts. After leaving the museum, allow some extra time for window shopping through the neighborhood where one can buy, sell or exchange exquisite wind or stringed instruments. This is one of the most asthetic small museums in Paris.

CERNUSHI

Type:	*Oriental*	Open:	*10-5:40 Daily*
Add:	*7, ave. Velasquez*	Closed:	*Mon & Holidays*
Tel:	*45.63.50.75*	Entry:	*12 Fr.*
Metro:	*Villiers*	Rating:	*****

There really was a Cernushi. He was an Italian financier/collector who lived during Napoleon's time. At the turn of the 19th century this charming villa was donated to the city of Paris by his heirs. It sits on the edge of one of Paris' most favored small parks, Monceau. Its interior design and contents make a fascinating center for Far Eastern art and antiques, some of which are attributable to Neolithic times. A fascinating assortment of animals of all sizes are about: horses, tigers, exotic birds and the inevitable dragon, all in sensuous bronzes. In contrast, there's an unusual salon upstairs with contemporary Chinese calligraphy, presided over by an immense fifth century Buddha. The most unusual feature of the Cernushi is that its bronzes are grouped out in open rooms, not behind glass. This visit could be combined with the Nissin-Camondo just around the corner.

NISSIM de CAMONDO

Type:	*Arts*	Open:	*10-12/2-5 Daily*
Add:	*63, rue de Monceau*	Closed:	*Mon Tues & Holidays*
Tel:	*45.63.26.32*	Entry:	*12 Fr.*
Metro:	*Villiers*	Rating:	****

Welcome to a warm and beautifully furnished villa, you are a privileged guest. Prepare yourself for an awesome sensation, for there is an elegant quality to the home of Moishe Camondo who passionately collected the objects of art, and donated the entire hotel to the city of Paris in memory of his son Nissim, who died in aerial combat in 1917. Every object within exemplifies an 18th century aristocratic style of utter simplicity. The stately portrait collection of preceding Camondo generations exudes an intimacy and personalness seldom seen. Notice also the perfect herringbone floors, the gem of an inner staircase and the small room in which their exquisite table service is displayed. Thanks to the Friends of the Committee for Camondo restoration goes on; the last surviving members of the Camondo legacy died in Auschwitz in 1944.

9th ARRONDISSEMENT

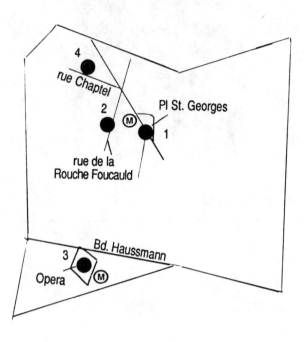

KEY	MUSEUM	PAGE
1.	Frederic Masson	57
2.	Gustave Moreau	58
3.	Opera	59
4.	Renan Scheffer	60

FREDERIC MASSON

Type:	*History*	Open:	*10-12/2-6 Daily*
Add:	*27, Place St. George*	Closed:	*Mondays*
Tel:	*48.78.14.33*	Entry:	10 Fr.
Metro:	*St. George*	Rating:	*

Frederic Masson was a French historian who held an insatiable fascination for Napoleon, his times and the happenings in his life. The small museum is on the second floor of Masson's former hotel and is composed of four salons which contain artifacts relating uniquely to The Grand Emperor, Napoleon Bonaparte. Masson gathered and collected medals, drawings, paintings, miniature figures, and uncountable memorabilia not only from France, but other European countries. The museum is actually under the auspices of the Library of the French Institute. Unless you`re particularly interested in the limited subject matter there's not much to be gained artistically at the Masson.

GUSTAVE MOREAU

Type: *Artist*
Add: *4, rue de la Rochefoucauld*
Tel: *48.74.38.50*
Metro: *St. George*

Open: *10-1/2-5 Daily*
Closed: *Monday & Tuesday*
Entry: *15 Fr.*
Rating: *

The works in this atelier are unusual at the very least. Moreau was a reclusive painter who lived in this hotel with his parents during the late 1800s. He is critized by few, admired by some and considered by others to have been a forerunner of the Fauvism style (Roualt, Matisse). There's mysticism and fantasy in every canvas; complex symbolism prevails. Most of the works are an erratic and erotic cross between mythology and religion, with languishing women and sensuous animals surrounded by lush landscapes. His varied drawings are numbered but untitled and it is impossible to discern dates. You will have to buy a guide to identify each work, and you're still on your own. Of course the reknowned spiral staircase to the uppermost floor must be climbed for still more unusual paintings. This visit, although fascinating, is confusing.

OPERA

Type:	*Music*	Open:	*10-5 Daily*
Add:	*1, Place Ch. Garnier*	Closed:	*Monday*
Tel:	*40.73.90.93*	Entry:	*6 Fr.*
Metro:	*Opera*	Rating:	*

To get to the small Opera Museum one must enter the Opera House, a 19th century neoclassical landmark and climb up to the second floor which is in itself well worth the price of admission. That grand marble staircase with its onyx and marble pillars and elegantly chandeliered tiers is an entry considered to be the ultimate in opulence and grandeur. Once within the museum you'll see mementos of operas, portraits of composers and small souvenirs. At one end there's a small wood paneled room in which original scores of operas are stacked to the ceiling, along with a dozen miniature sets of opera scenes. The one thing wrong here is that there is no sense of order. This museum will be moved to Opera Bastille in 1988 and the existing Opera House will fortunately remain where it is to become the home of the elegant Paris Opera Ballet.

RENAN SCHEFFER

Type:	*Artist*	Open:	*10-5:40 Daily*
Add:	*16, rue Chaptal*	Closed:	*Monday*
Tel:	*45.74.95.38*	Entry:	*9 Fr.*
Metro:	*St. George*	Rating:	***

Ary Scheffer, a highly sophisticated artist, lived here for almost thirty years during the early 1800's where he completed most of his sensuous portraits and drawings. The small museum is a charming hotel, well restored and simply kept, presenting his works and his circle of friends: Chopin, George Sand, Delacroix, Liszt, and Ingres. There's a George Sand room containing drawings and paintings of her family, personal adornments and other memorabilia, another for Franz Liszt, an excitingly dramatic figure. Look for the fascinating group portrait of Liszt and his esoteric friends: Dumas Pere, Sand, Hugo, Paganini and Rosini. With Chopin music barely heard in the background this makes for one of the best of the small museums, from the tiny courtyard at the entry to the rear gardens. It's also hardly visited.

10th ARRONDISSEMENT

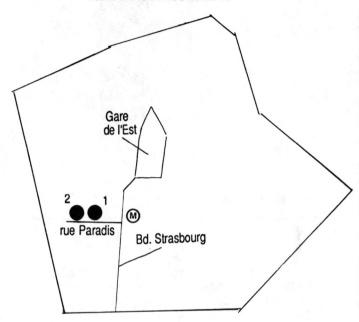

KEY	MUSEUM	PAGE

L'AFFICHE et PUBLICITE

Type: *Social*
Add: *19, rue de Parodis*
Tel: *42.46.13.09*
Entry: *16f*

Open: *Daily 12-6*
Closed: *Monday's*
Rating: **

Before entering this museum you might spend a few moments standing across from it in contemplation of the facade. It's done in ceramic/mosaic, reminiscent of a turn of the century theatre and, if you look hard enough, the name of Boulancer et Cie, who were makers of faience, is hand crafted into the design. The colorful and unique motif continues on into the courtyard and up the staircase to the entrance. The one-room museum supports itself by radiant poster exhibitions, all well attended. In addition to an incredible assortment of picture post cards, the tiny store off to one corner boasts a collection of more than 40,000 posters, some dating back to the 18th century, and sells more posters than any one place in Paris. There's also a tiny cinema room where films are shown on the current exhibition. Combine this visit with Baccarat, just up the street.

BACCARAT

Type:	*Social*	Open:	*9-6 Daily*
Add:	*30, rue de Paradis*	Closed:	*Saturday & Sunday*
Tel:	*47.70.64.30*	Entry:	*Free*
Metro:	*Chateau d'Eau*	Rating:	****

Enter through the large courtyard and up the broad stairs where
the entry on the first floor must be appreciated, that enormous
figure fabricated from thousands of pieces of assorted colored
crystal! The museum is really a showroom featuring the
celebrated manufacturer's table crystal of exquisite quality,
some selling for thousands of dollars a set. According to
Baccarat, each wine is at least entitled to its own goblet.
There's a room off to the side containing museum pieces of
infinite perfection. If you're looking for bargains this is not
the place to shop. Rue Paradis and neighboring streets are in
fact the center for crystal and porcelain where, since most
shops claim to be duty free, prices are more realistic. During
your enraptured visit to Baccarat do not overlook those assorted
chandeliers, each worth a fortune and priced accordingly. Ah,
for the good life.

11th ARRONDISSEMENT

KEY	MUSEUM	PAGE
1.	Edith Piaf	65

EDITH PIAF

Type:	*Individual*	Open:	*Afternoons Only by*
Add:	*5, rue Crespin-du-Gast*		*Telephone Appointment*
Tel:	*43.55.52.72*	Closed:	*Sat Sun & Holidays*
Metro:	*Menilmontant*	Rating:	***
Entry:	10 Fr.		

The entry to the museum could be easily missed. Look for the plaque to the left of the doorway and the gloomy entrance, then through the courtyard and up the stairs. The museum, two rooms that were Piaf's private apartment, contains photographs, programs, notices and souvenirs of her development from a ragtag, undisciplined street singer of Pigalle into a mature entertainer, enchanting audiences in the cabarets of Paris and the world. Her life was a series of brief, tumultuous love affairs. She was a heavy drinker, her health gradually detiorated, she ran into debt. Still lonely, frail and sickly the little sparrow died in 1963 on the same day as her dear friend Jean Cocteau. The unforgettable, diminutive Edith Piaf is still worshipped and adored, for she epitomized the nostalgia that is France.

12th ARRONDISSEMENT

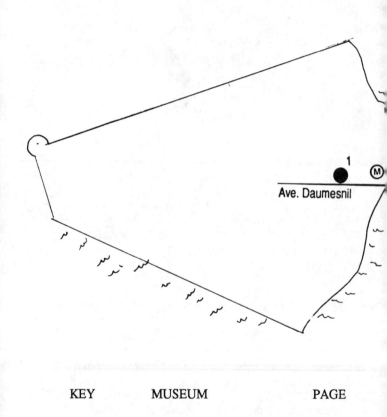

Ave. Daumesnil

AFRICAINES et OCEANIENS

Type:	*Arts*	Open:	*10-12/2-5:30*
Add:	*293, ave Daumesnil*	Closed:	*Tuesday*
Tel:	*43.43.14.54*	Entry:	*12 Fr.*
Metro:	*Port Doree*	Rating:	****

You can't miss this enormous museum which occupies an entire city block. It's in the southeasternmost part of the 12th Arrondissement and takes quite a long time to reach from any part of Paris. If I had to choose only one word to describe this museum, I would say "colossal". It is also the most varied show of African art you will see anywhere, even in Africa, from places you've probably never heard of. For an added attraction there are a number of rooms with exotic art from the Pacific Islands and a special salon of Australian Aboriginal culture, unfortunately undated. Downstairs the aquarium, with its mind boggling assortment of fish and turtles will astound you - why, they've even got a crocodile pool complete with a community of crocs! To round out your perfect day, the world famous Bois de Vincennes and its zoo is a mere two blocks away.

15th ARRONDISSEMENT

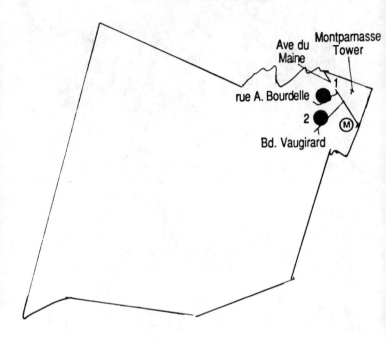

KEY	MUSEUM	PAGE

EMILE ANTOINE BOURDELLE

Type: *Artist*   Open: *10-5:40 Daily*
Add: *16, rue Antoine*   Closed: *Mon & Holidays*
Bourdelle   Entry: *9 Fr.*
Tel: *45.48.67.27*   Rating: ******
Metro: *Montparnasse Bienvenue*

You can't miss locating this one, the small front garden
holding no less than eighty sculptured figures, heads and
animals complete with winding paths. Emile Bourdelle, called
Antoine since his wife's name was Cleopatra, was a sculptor
of relatively small reknown in the late 1880's and early 1900's.
If you detect a subtle Rodin influence you are correct: they
were colleagues. This restored hotel is where Antoine lived
and worked, completing more than 1,000 sensuous pieces from
small heads to larger than life figures. Salon after salon yields
exquisite sculptures and still more upstairs. The inner
courtyard gardens are overgrown with yet more enormous
sculptures. A number of oils and pastels are scattered about,
but the quality of Bourdelle's paintings do not compare to his
sculptures. Don't forget to stroll through those sculpture
gardens on your way out.

POSTE

Type: *Social*
Add: *34, Bd de Vaugirard*
Tel: 43.20.15.30
Metro: *Montparnasse Bienvenue*

Open: *10-5 Daily*
Closed: *Sun & Holidays*
Entry: 5 Fr.
Rating: ****

The museum is easily found in the huge Post Office building located in the center of bustling Montparnasse and just behind the tower. Start on the fifth floor and work your way down through fifteen salons to the first floor. It's the history of mail service from the origins of writing in 4500 B.C. to the present, the chronology of stamp design, stamp engraving, stamp printing techniques, and weight measuring devices, a fascinating visit for philatellists. You'll follow the development of courier systems via bicycle, ship, train and plane. There's a mail box display, mailman costumes, a presentation of telecommunications and a room filled with rare, prized stamps. This museum, hardly noticed and scarcely visited, is an example of how, given time, energy and money, a museum can present information in an intelligent manner.

16th ARRONDISSEMENT.

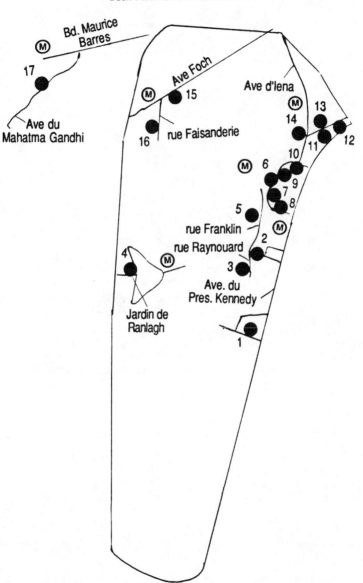

RADIO FRANCE

Type: *Social*
Add: *116, Ave du President Kennedy*
Tel: *42.30.30.12*
Metro: *Passy*

Open: *10-12/2-5 Daily*
Closed: *Monday*
Entry: *7 Fr.*
Rating: **

The communications building, a 15 story tower standing in the center of a concrete circle overlooking the Seine, is quite impressive. The Radio Museum within conducts tours every two hours, French only, with an interesting walk through the recording and broadcasting studios and technical exhibits. Transmission of sound waves and radio communication as we know it today became a reality after the arrival of electricity around 1832. This self-contained center, through its well presented displays traces the growth of radio, phonographs, microphones, television, transistors, tubes and chips. Musical festivals and concerts are seasonally held in the south portion of the building. The National Philharmonic Orchestra and the Paris Choral Group record and perform both in the Grande Salle and Concert Hall.

VIN

Type:	*Social*	Open:	*12-6 Daily*
Add:	*rue des Eaux*	Closed:	*Monday*
Tel:	*45.25.63.26*	Entry:	*20 Fr.*
Metro:	*Passy*	Rating:	**

During the 15th and 16th centuries this was the site of an
abbey and vineyard, and is now a part of Paris' fashionable
16th arrondissement. The museum serves as a display of as
complete a study and historical center for wine as can be found
anywhere, complete with damp cave aroma. There are
thousands of varieties of wine from different origins, displays
of wine making, miscellaneous memorabilia of the world of
wine, from assorted porcelain figures to fancy corkscrews to
proper barrelling to the proper method of sipping. An extra
touch is added with occasional scenes of wax figures engaged
in social proprieties of wine consumption. Yes, that is
Napoleon drinking his favorite wine, vintage unknown. Save
the testing, tasting and buying for the end of the visit.

BALZAC

Type:	*Individual*	Open:	*10-5:40 Daily*
Add:	*47, rue Raynouard*	Closed:	*M, T, & Holidays*
Tel:	*42.24.56.38*	Entry:	*10 Fr.*
Metro:	*Passy*	Rating:	*

This was the home and atelier of Balzac during the last ten years of his life. It is filled with portraits of him, his family and friends, some sculptures, posters, illustrations, engravings, photographs and mementos, plus showcases of letters and manuscripts. Balzac had great literary influence upon the world. His works (the most celebrated is The Human Comedy) have been translated into eight languages and he remains on a level of prominence with Dumas, Zola and Hugo. He was a dashing figure, somewhat bulky, who draped himself in a monk's frock and was immortalized by Rodin's enormous sculpture. Apparently he was was portrayed as a buffoon, a Bacchus, a spendthrift, and realized few honors during his lifetime. There's a small cinema room downstairs which shows a 15 -minute film on his life and work. For some extra insights, visit his red velvet study. Balzac was fifty years old when he died in Paris in 1850.

MARMOTTAN

Type:	*Artist*	Open:	*10-5:30*
Add:	*2, rue Louis Boily*	Closed:	*Monday*
Tel:	*42.24.07.02*	Entry:	*20 Fr.*
Metro:	*Muette*	Rating:	****

Leave Metro Muette and cross one of Paris' enchanting parks, Ranleigh Gardens, to arrive at the town house of Monet and his Friends. The entire main floor holds paintings, tapestries, sculptures and furnishings of the 18th century. The upstairs has just been beautifully restored. Here Monet predominates surrounded by his friends; Sisley, Pissarro, Renoir, and Morrisot. Be sure to notice the uniquely inlaid floors of the small round rooms. And of course downstairs visit the Monet Gallery, where his spectacular water lilies of purple and orchid, unlike any colors in the world of art, will stun you. Read those modest letters so painfully intimate on the subject of his overdue commissions. Isn't it difficult to believe he was compelled to request payment for these masterpieces? Marmottan is not glamourosly decorated, but what good fortune to find so very much of a very good thing.

CLEMENCEAU

Type: *Individual*
Add: *8, rue Franklin*
Tel: *45.20.43.41*
Metro: *Passy*

Open: *2-5 Tu Th Sa Su*
Entry: *10 Fr.*
Rating: ✱✱

Georges Clemenceu was a distinguished statesman and highly respected man of letters in addition to having been a successful author and playwright. This was his residence, preserved intact since his last days in 1929. During his journalistic period he printed voluminous articles on human rights, war and peace, justice and patriotism, and was an active colleague of Emile Zola during the Dreyfus affair. The museum contains medals of honor and prestigious awards bestowed upon him by reknowned world leaders. You'll see him in photos taken at the signing of the Versailles Treaty in which he participated. Look in one of the upstairs vitrines; there's a Clemenceau book written in 1898 and illustrated by none other than H. de Toulouse Lautrec! And if you noticed the many small Monets you have astutely discovered that the two enjoyed a profound and lasting relationship (see Giverny).

PALAIS de CHAILLOT

Type:	*General*	Open:	*Daily*
Add:	*Palais de Chaillot*	Entry:	*Free*
Tel:	*45.53.74.39*	Rating:	****
Metro:	*Trocadero*		

The Palace stands directly across the Seine facing the Eiffel Tower - an imposing structure with two armlike wings sweeping out from an open semicircular terrace. Spreading down towards the Seine are sloped gardens, fountains and golden statues where crowds gather to sun worship or loll about. It's one of Paris' major tourist attractions, partly on its own merits and partly for its proximity to the Eiffel Tower. Below the central terrace is the huge Theatre de Chaillot which serves as concert hall, cultural center, and theatre. There's also an Aquarium. Above at street level the main wings contain four museums: Monuments Francais and Cinema in the east wing; Marine and l'Homme in the west wing, all described in the following chapters. Each has its own time schedule and admission price and all are entered from the north doors facing Place du Trocadero.

MONUMENTS FRANCAIS

Type: *History*

Add: *Palais de Chaillot*

Tel: *47.27.35.74*

Metro: *Trocadero*

Open: *9:45-12:30/2-5:45 Daily*

Closed: *Tuesday*

Entry: *12 Fr.*

Rating: ****

The importance of architecture and its relation to civilization, or vice versa, was woefully overlooked until this fascinating museum came into being. According to evidence here, there were two Renaissances in architecture, the first from 1495 to 1530, and the second from 1530 to 1575, two relatively brief moments in the grand time plan of civilization. The history of architecture and sculpture is explained through full models or fragments of French monuments which are perfect replicas chronologically arranged with descriptions of that particular time and category. Every salon is vast and extremely well done. An incredible sculpture display on the second floor is accompanied by some very exciting frescoes. You don't have to love architecture to enjoy this museum, you'll simply get your money's worth.

CINEMA, HENRI LANGLOIS

Type: *General*   Open: *Guided Visits Only*
Add: *Palais de Chaillot*   *Daily*
Tel: *45.53.74.39*   Closed: *Monday*
Metro: *Trocadero*   Entry: *20 Fr.*
          Rating: ******

The museum owes its existence to Henri Langlois, a wealthy
French patron of the arts, who wanted to present to the world a
memento of the history of cinema from its origins up to the
present. He has succeeded. Starting with early 19th century
marionettes, the viewer is taken on a chronological tour of
every phase of cinematography since its inception. Every
exhibit relates solely to the creation and development of the
film industry, its struggles, conflicts and accomplishments.
Dozens of rooms display heroes and heroines, creators and
stars, villains, sets, costumes, posters, original cameras, and
technical theories of projection. This is an incredible
conglomeration of fragments of fantasy, coupled with shrewd
visions of a highly popular form of entertainment. Tours are
flamboyantly conducted in French and last two hours. What an
exciting place for movie buffs!

MUSEE de la MARINE

Type:	*Military*	Open:	*10-6 Daily*
Add:	*Palais de Chaillot*	Closed:	*Tuesday*
Tel:	*45.53.31.70*	Entry:	*12Fr.*
Metro:	*Trocadero*	Rating:	***

There are more ship models of incredible assortment and fine quality here than anywhere else in the world. Practically every model is an original. You might say this museum is the complete history of the French Navy and Merchant Marine, from ships to cannons to mermaids covering more than three centuries of French maritime history. In addition to hundreds of engravings and maps there are a multitude of paintings of some of France's most formidable sea battles. Other subjects covered are origins and current modes of navigation, trade and commerce on the seas, international fishing, topography of the sea floors, heroes of the sea, war, nuclear propulsion and on and on. The workshop downstairs restores models fastidiously faithful to their original designs. This is in no way an art museum, it is totally academic.

MUSEE de l'HOMME

Type:	*Natural History*	Open:	*10-6 Daily*
Add:	*Palais de Chaillot*	Closed:	*Tuesday*
Tel:	*45.05.70.60*	Entry:	*15 Fr.*
Metro:	*Trocadero*	Rating:	**

This museum is somewhat better than other museums of
natural history, perhaps because of its vastness. Two floors
are literally filled with prehistoric anthropology and ethnology.
It is not only a museum, it's a teaching and research center of
natural history with its own huge theatre for documentary
films and lectures. Look for the Goddess Venus shown in full
glory, along with a curious display on Chananism (that's the
study of communication with an invisible world) on the upper
floor, with its strange ritualistic curios and costumes, oddly
enough popular in Siberia. The exciting Salon de Musique
must be visited to appreciate the impact of music on all levels
and times of civilization. And if you're lucky enough to arrive
at the right moment, you might be treated to an unusual
concert.

PALAIS de TOKYO

Type: *General*
Add: *11, Ave du President Wilson*
Tel: *47.23.36.53*
Metro: *Iena*

Open: *9:45−5:15 Daily*
Closed: *Tuesday*
Entry: *18 Fr.*
Rating: **

Originally, the Palais de Tokyo, built for the 1937 World's Fair, was the official Paris Museum of Modern Art until the Georges Pompidou opened in the late 1970`s. At that time the majority of the contemporary art went to the Pompidou, the remaining works to the new Musee d'Orsay (1986). All this leaves the remaining space still to be accounted for, i.e., the entire east wing of the Palace. A small portion on the lower level now houses the permanent National Center of Photography, which shows some pretty unusual camera techniques of current photographers. Speculation has it that this space would be perfectly suited as an exposition hall, per the Grand Palais. There seems to be something seriously lacking here, though. The atmosphere lacks spontaneity and it is rather listless.

ART MODERNE VILLE de PARIS

Type: *Arts*
Add: *11, Ave du President Wilson*
Tel: *47.23.61.27*
Metro: *Iena*

Open: *10-5:40 Daily*
Closed: *Monday*
Entry: *18 Fr.*
Rating: ****

If you were planning to open a museum of 20th century art, there's nothing like the !luxury of gigantesque salons which is precisely what this museum has, perfect for the accommodation of some enormous canvasses. The museum occupies the entire west wing of the Palais de Tokyo. This is contemporary art at its best and very exciting at that. It's a good place to get to know Georges Roualt, Cezanne, and a number of modern painters. There's a fine display of African and Pacific Island sculptures and some Matisse cut-outs, and if you enjoy theatre, cinema, dance or good jazz, scheduled concerts are held in the two lower auditoriums. For a Sunday afternoon the childrens' museum is downstairs, plus an extraordinary salon of 19th and 20th century furniture which will take your breath away. It's an absolute must.

MODE et du COSTUME (GALIERA)

Type: *Fashion*
Add: *Palais Galiera*
   10, Ave. Pierre Serbie
Tel: *47.20.85.46*
Metro: *Iena*

Open: *10-5:40 Daily*
Closed: *Monday*
Entry: *18 Fr.*
Rating: ******

The museum is an Italian Renaissance palace built during the
19th century, and its architecture is a museum unto itself. The
palace was lived in by the Duchess of Galliera, thus its name.
A portion of the permanent collection belonged to her and her
genteel circle. The remainder shows fashion for men, women
and children of elegant standing during the 18th, 19th, and
20th centuries and includes a collection of equally glamorous
accessories. Temporary exhibitions related to fashions from
other epochs are continually held, done in taste apropos to the
very finest haute maisons de couture. A stroll through the
gardens out back is a good idea. There are wide paths, flower
beds, sculptures and benches. Galiera rates a ten.

GUIMET

Type:	*Oriental*	Open:	*9:45-12/1:30-5:45 Daily*
Add:	*6, Place d'Iena*	Closed:	*Tuesdays*
Tel:	*47.23.61.65*	Entry:	*12 Fr.*
Metro:	*Iena*	Rating:	******

The Museum of Asian Art is what Guimet is about and
magnificent is the collection, probably the best in Europe.
Emile Guimet, an explorer/industrialist, collected the contents
of this remarkable place and late in the 19th century donated it
to the city of Paris. Its three floors exude a totally exotic
atmosphere, showing from 1,000 B.C. to 18th century
Buddhas, statues, an immense spectrum of Asian art from
Japan, Thailand, Nepal, Turkey, Laos, Burma and the
Indonesian Islands, plus a gorgeous display from Tibet.
Besides all this, Guimet is a center for Asian research and
study with a library to match. Gallery after gallery of
sculptures, ceramics and jewels will fascinate you. This is a
first-class museum, a sleeper, and should be visited.

ENNERY

Type:	*Oriental*	Open:	*2-5 Sun. Thurs.*
Add:	*59, Avenue Foch*	Closed:	*Holidays & August*
Tel:	*45.53.57.96*	Entry:	*10 Fr.*
Metro:	*Port Dauphine*	Rating:	***

Adolph d'Ennery, a 19th century novelist, and his wife were passionately devoted to Oriental art. During the years they lived in this opulent mansion they bought anything and everything of Far Eastern cultural and religious art. The museum, although in need of restoration, is of elegant standing in an equally elegant part of Paris. The showcases are exquisite objects of art and contain thousands of the finest figurines seen anywhere; all appointments are equally magnificent. The galleries are filled with porcelains, ivories, and jades. If you're not intimidated by a myriad of vitrines crammed full of small art, you will enjoy this visit. It doesn't matter that practically all the miniatures are not identified. Don't miss those huge bronze, wood and porcelain animals on guard throughout.

CONTREFACON

Type: *Social*
Add: *16, rue de la Faisanderie*
Tel: *45.01.51.11*
Metro: *Porte Dauphine*

Open: *9:30-5 Daily*
Closed: *Sunday*
Entry: *Free*
Rating: ******

Here is a one room museum which shows counterfeit items of every description, from fake wine cisterns of the Roman Empire up to trendy, high priced signature apparel and accessories of today. The museum was founded in 1951 in order to bring to light the enormous losses suffered by legitimate businesses as a result of skilled counterfeitors. In some instances lawsuits have been brought about, however, counterfeitors still proliferate. From high quality boissons to perfumes, handbags, watches, shoes and luggage, the packaging is almost perfectly duplicated. Displays show the genuine article and alongside its ingenious copy. Test yourself by carefully comparing the two models. It is practically impossible to discern the difference. Amusing but confusing!

ARTS et TRADITIONS POPULAIRE

Type: *Social*
Add: *6, Ave du*
Mahatma Gandhi
Tel: *47.47.69.80*
Metro: *Sablons*

Open: *10-5:15 Daily*
Closed: *Tuesday*
Entry: *15 Fr.*
Rating: *****

I can tell you what this museum is not. It is not the
conventional museum of natural history, but rather a museum
of the cultural and sociological development of rural French
habitations and traditional living standards during the 19th
century. It's in a brand new building located in the
northwesternmost corner of the 16th Arrondissement and takes
a good bit of time to reach. The museum has costumes and
modes of dress, music and entertainment, the sport of hunting,
mountain life, country life, furniture and furnishings, and
family social structures. Even the circus is displayed as a
structured social form. There's a section on mythological and
supernatural beliefs such as crystal balls, horoscopes, cards,
satanic worship, and magic potions. All are well presented,
however very few displays are dated.

90

17th ARRONDISSEMENT

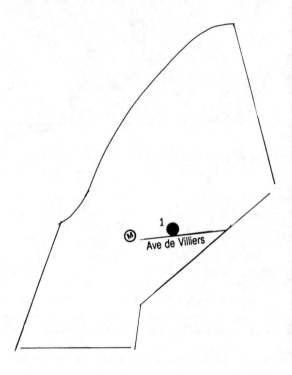

KEY	MUSEUM	PAGE
1.	Henner	91

HENNER

Type:	*Artist*	Open:	*10-12/2-5 Daily*
Add:	*43, Avenue de Villiers*	Closed:	*Monday*
Tel:	*47.63.42.73*	Entry:	*12 Fr.*
Metro:	*Malesherbes*	Rating:	**

The museum contains four floors of a unique collection of works of the prolific but little known French artist, Jean-Jacques Henner, who lived during the mid 1800's. He was fascinated by feminine nudes and oddly enough, studies of figures reclining in death. But his best pieces are the glowing portraits in exquisite oils, the majority of which are silhouettes. The hotel itself has an interesting interior design. The small salons are placed one directly above the other and are reached by climbing a tiny staircase - or using an equally tiny elevator. The room at the very top not only has some of his drawings, etchings and water colors done during his two year stay in Italy but some of the best nude studies you'll see anywhere. The museum, scarcely noticed, is highly polished and lovingly looked after by dedicated Friends of J.J. Henner.

92

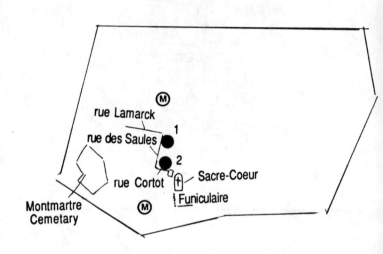

KEY	MUSEUM	PAGE
1.	Juif	93
2.	Montmartre	94

ART JUIF

Type:	*General*	Open:	*3-5 Daily*
Add:	*42, rue des Saules*	Closed:	*Fri & Sat*
Tel:	*42.57.84.15*	Entry:	*10 Fr.*
Metro:	*Lamark-Caulaincourt*	Rating:	***

The small building houses the Merkaz of Montmartre, which is a Hebrew center of study for both children and adults. Climb the stairs up to the third floor to find, in this tiny museum, sensitive and touching Jewish manuscripts, religious memorabilia and works of art, all beautifully presented. Each rare display has been gathered from synagogues of Europe, Africa, and the Middle East and all are contained in four small rooms. For instance, one room holds religious paintings and mosaics from the 5th to the 10th century and in another there's a portion of an early Hebrew fresco taken from a 1st century Mesopotamian synagogue. There are several wooden models of synagogues which doubled as fortresses during the 17th and 18th centuries. It is brought to light that every synagogue in Poland and Lithuania was destroyed by the Nazis during World War II. Small wonder that every precious article is lovingly displayed.

MONTMARTRE

Type:	*History*	Open:	*2:30-5:30 Daily*
Add:	*12, rue Cortot*	Closed:	*Monday*
Tel:	*46.06.61.11*	Entry:	*10 Fr.*
Metro:	*Abesses*	Rating:	*

You're going to have to look hard for this one, even with the aid of your map. Not only is it small in size, but its facade is somewhat undistinguishable. From the Metro take the Funiculaire to the top of the hill which is Sacre Coeur and follow the "Musee" signs. According to these nostalgic paintings, drawings and documents, Montmartre was a self contained world unto itself with its own governing system and distinct social values and at one time considered ceceding from Paris. No one is certain whether its location is the reason, but in a sense Montmartre still considers itself a separate entity with its biting, earthy mood clinging to the past when Toulouse and his rebelliously intellectual colleagues flourished. The music and arts shown here reinforce Montmartre's vigorously Bacchinalian reputation during the 19th century. A lunch stop at the square will top off your day.

19th ARRONDISSEMENT

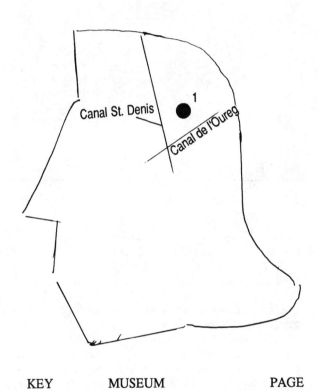

KEY	MUSEUM	PAGE
1.	La Villette	96

LA VILLETTE

Type:	*General*	Open:	*Year Round*
Add:	*Parc de la Villette*	Entry:	*Free*
Tel:	*42.45.66.00*	Rating:	***
Metro:	*Villette*		

This project is one of Paris' (and the French Government's) most ambitious and expensive undertakings, costing billions of francs and years of planning. Once a former slaughterhouse, its very size puts the Pompidou, which is one tenth the size, back into the little league. According to public opinion these plans place La Villette on an audacious scale, a new summit of splendiferousness and exhibitionism. La Geode, the giant stainless steel sphere which sits in a tranquil pool of water and has been designated as the symbol of La Villette, shows an exciting space film every hour to a packed house at 40 francs entry. La Grande Hall, seating 15,000, holds shows, spectacles, live performances and expositions (Salons). The Museum of Science and Technology promises to be the largest science museum in the world, covering 7 1/2 acres. The Zenith Rock Music Hall features current rock stars, drawing Paris' trendy young set. There's an imaginative playground/park complete with a fun slide, and the Reading Play Center for children is unmatched. The complex is so spread out it would take a full day just to cover all sections. Future plans include an International Conference Center, a Research Center, Science Clubs, a City of Music and Concert Hall, a Cine Club, a National Conservatory, a Planetarium, and any number of restaurants. Too bad it takes an interminably long time to reach, and all this very obviously built over what one could swear are medieval ruins. Be mindful that Sunday is family day at La Villette, and you know what that means.

OUTER PARIS
(Giverny)

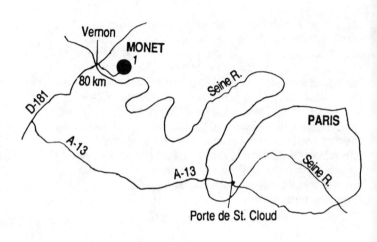

KEY	MUSEUM	PAGE
1.	Monet	99

GIVERNY

Type: *Artist*
Add: *Vernon*

Open: *House 10-12/2-6*
Gardens 10-6 Daily
Closed: *Monday*
Entry: *25 Fr.*
Rating: ****

The government of France, together with generous contributions from Friends of Monet have preserved his home and gardens in their original state. Although this museum is not within Paris itself, it deserves mention beyond honorable. On arriving, the first impact is one of complete tranquility. But first to the house, a two-story pink stucco with green shutters. The entry, known as the main salon, was where guests were received and is now used as a gallery for copies of his works and the museum store. (By the way, none of Monet's original paintings are here, they're all copies.) Look for the bust of Monet done by Rodin and across the room, one of Georges Clemenceau, Monet's dear friend, who persuaded Monet to donate his water lilies to France (see Clemenceau). The house is furnished simply and with an obvious lack of ornateness. Monet was a fastidious collector of Oriental prints and engravings. These are the sole wall adornments we see, interrupted by an occasional photo of the Monet family. (Notice the small ceramic box on the vestibule wall.) Vases and pots of fresh flowers are in all the rooms. Ultimately joyous is the bright yellow dining room with its matching Oriental prints and Monet's specially designed faiences. Next is the unbelievable blue and white ceramin kitchen, done in typically Rouen fashion, again for Monet alone. The years at Giverny were spent painting mainly outdoors; it was Monet who designed his gardens, which have as great an appeal to haute tourism as the interior of his home. This is where his immortal lily ponds and sunlit figures were painted. As you wander through the maze of color, look for the stream which runs through the gardens. It's a tributary of the very same Seine we strolled along in Paris. Although Monet modestly claimed to be interested only in his adored gardens, he was regarded by his colleagues to be the ultimate Grand Maitre d'Impressionism, the Master of still life, landscapes, and figures, and rightfully so. Alas, although Monet developed cataracts in his later years, he realized wealth and recognition thanks to some astute international art collectors. Only after his death did France appreciate his greatness. The museum is about one hour's drive northwest of Paris, unless you prefer the train. It's the Paris/Rouen line, Gare St. Lazare. This is undoubtedly one of the best days you'll ever spend in any museum. Top it off with lunch in the country.

OUTER PARIS
(Versailles)

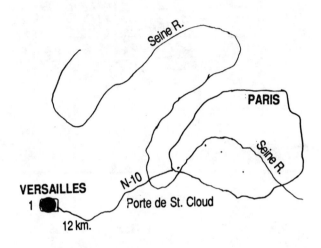

KEY	MUSEUM	PAGE
1.	Palais de Versailles	102

VERSAILLES

Type:	*History*	Open:	*9:45-5:30 Daily*
Add:	*Palais de Versailles*	Closed:	*Monday*
		Entry:	*25 Fr.*
		Rating:	****

It's pretty certain that even if you moved at breakneck pace, seeing Versailles in one day is not only unrealistic, it is out of the question. It is surely the largest and most ornate palace in the world, reputedly having taken 50 years and billions of francs to complete during the mid 1600's. At that time France was the richest, most powerful, most cultured nation in Europe. Some critics still maintain that Versailles is ostentatious and pretentious. Nevertheless, other European rulers copied Versailles in smaller versions for themselves. As for your visit, Versailles can be broken down into three divisions which might facilitate proper appreciation: the Grands Appartements, the Petit Appartements, and the Grands Eaux Musicales (Fountain Concert). Entry for the three can be purchased in one combined ticket. I would recommend timing your visit to coincide with the fountain spectacle held only on Sunday afternoons at 3 p.m.and lasts for 90 minutes. After visiting the stunning interior of the Palace, you will assemble outside in the gardens and await a concert of classical Louis XIV music, at which moment each of the 24 magnificent fountains explodes into a showering display, no two alike. Guests then promenade up, down, and around the broad avenues, through the parks, woods, canals, statues and flower beds and at each turn discover yet another fountain. The gardens were created by one of the greatest landscape designers of all times, Le Notre. What a way to spend a Sunday afternoon. Thank you Louis XIV, Sun King, le Dauphin, this grand palace is your enduring monument (and don't forget le Petit Trianon).

APPENDIX

ARTIST Museums - Although the majority of Artists are of French nationality, a number of those not did live for some period of time in France.

ARTS Museums - Contain conventional paintings and sculptures, either of Classical, Modern, or Impressionistic style.

FASHION Museums - Deserve special mention because of their extraordinary creativity and connection to Paris, which enjoys undeniable honors as one of the foremost trendsetters of fashion.

GENERAL Museums - Have widely varied contents of arts and sculptures and may cater only to temporary exhibitions or specific subject matters not found in other museums.

HISTORY Museums - Apply to those museums giving insight into matters pertaining to either historical Paris or historical France.

INDIVIDUAL Museums - Honor persons related to the arts other than arts, e.g., writers, statesmen, entertainers, etc.

MILITARY Museums - Pertain naturally to all branches of the French armed forces from all times.

MUSIC Museums - Might contain some art but only as it applies to the instruments, theories, and practices of music within that museum.

NATURAL HISTORY Museums - Show the natural sciences of creation, evolution, and civilization involving plants, animals and the universe.

ORIENTAL Museums - Contain only objects of art of Oriental or Far Eastern origins.

SCIENCE Museums - Exhibit both theoretical and proven discoveries of technical or general scientific interest.

SOCIAL Museums - A number of these contain neither arts nor sciences. Their contents relate strictly to social practices.

ARTIST MUSEUMS

Delacroix, Eugene	35
Giverny (Monet)	99
Henner, J.J	91
Marmottan (Monet)	76
Moreau, Gustave	58
Picasso, Pablo	19
Renan Scheffer	60
Rodin, P. Auguste	44
Zadkine, O	37

ARTS MUSEUMS

Arts Africaines et Oceaniens	67
Arts Decoratifs	2
Art Moderne, Ville de Paris	84
Cognac Jay	11
D'Orsay	39
Jeu de Paume	6
Louvre	7
Nissim de Camondo	55
Orangerie	9
Pompidou, Georges	27
Sculpture Plein Air	33

FASHION MUSEUMS

Arts de la Mode	3
Mode et du Costume (Galiera)	85

GENERAL MUSEUMS

Bricard de la Serrure	14
Chaillot, Palais de	78
Chasse et de la Nature	15
Cinema, Henri Langlois	80
Grand Palais	50
Grevin	4
Jaquemart Andre	52

108

INDEX

AFTERWORD

This book was designed to travel along with you. Keep it
constantly at your fingertips, for it is your personal guide. I
have provided separate pages for NOTES. Use them freely
during your trip. You'll turn to them after your return for
reminders of your unforgettable art experience.

I hope that, through MUSEUMS OF PARIS I have provided
you with rich and rewarding insights and a finer understanding
of the Arts.

For additional copies of MUSEUMS OF PARIS, please use
the following application. Order now for prompt, immediate
delivery.

NAME_____

ADDRESS_____

CITY_____STATE_____ZIP__

I AM ENCLOSING A CHECK ($9.95 per copy plus $1.00
for postage)

_____ copies of MUSEUMS OF PARIS $9.95

_____ copies of SMALL MUSEUMS OF THE
FRENCH RIVIERA $9.95

*MUSEUMS OF FLORENCE will be published in
September 1987

ELDAN PRESS   1259 El Camino #288   Menlo Park, CA 94025

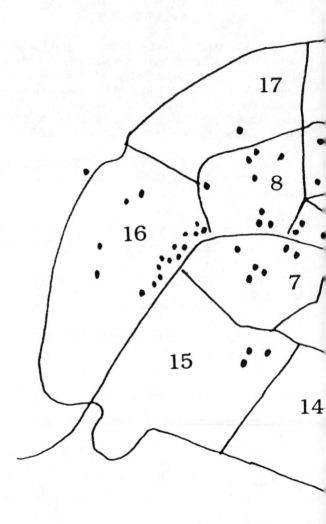